D1779286

Poets of Darkness

Credit: Malcolm Jay Wilson

Poets of Darkness

by
James B. Goode

PUBLISHED FOR
THE UNIVERSITY OF MISSISSIPPI
CENTER FOR THE STUDY
OF SOUTHERN CULTURE
BY THE
UNIVERSITY PRESS
OF MISSISSIPPI
Jackson
1981

Other Books by the Author

Appalachian Mountain Mother 1969

The Whistle and the Wind 1971

Copyright 1981 By James B. Goode
Manufactured in the United States of America
All Rights Reserved
This volume has been sponsored and authorized
by the University of Mississippi Center for the
Study of Southern Culture

Library of Congress Cataloging in Publication Data

Goode, James B   1948-
   Poets of darkness.

   1. Coal mines and mining—Kentucky—Poetry.
2. Kentucky—Poetry. I. Title.
PS3557.O54P6   811'.54   80-29653
ISBN 0-87805-133-3

To all who go down in the mines

But Especially

For Mike Simpson

A Friend

Who Didn't Return.

"Today the Blackest Roses Bloom"

Contents

Acknowledgments 9

Preface 11

Poets of Darkness   15

Wednesday, June 7, 1978
 Today the Blackest Roses Bloom   16

Late Afternoon   18

Song of Sorrow   22

Her Bear Branch Man   24

Like the Last Good-Bye   25

A Funeral For Five of the Thirty-Eight Dead   26

Coal Miner's Graveyard   27

For Those Who Sleep   28

When Coal Miners Come Home   29

They Come to Dig Coal   30

Black Labyrinths   31

Coal Car Riders   32

Photographic Essay   33

Where Fossil Ferns Are Constellations   41

The Coal Camp Sleeps   42

To A Man With A Small Truck Mine   43

Boom Town Boys   45

Boom Town Poolroom   46

Roadhouses   47

The Ballad of the Harlan County
 Criminal Justice System   48

Ballad For A Union Man   51

100 Days and Counting . . .   53

Plug-Uglies in Harlan   54

The Value of It All   55

Ghost Town of Appalachia   56

Paradox   57

Appalachian Snake Handlers   58

Spider   59

Pentecost in Coal Town   62

C Seam Shovel   63

Cold Beer on Hot Harlan County Nights   64

Acknowledgments

THANKS TO: Benham Coal Company for a generous donation of historic photographs and precious time.

Victor Howard for his generosity and foresight in donating almost 90,000 historic negatives and prints.

Malcolm Jay Wilson of Appalachian Images, Cumberland, Kentucky, for superb photographs of coal miners.

Bill Ferris for believing in the idea.

James Dollarhide and Lisa Saylor who lent technical assistance and tolerated my perfectionist personality.

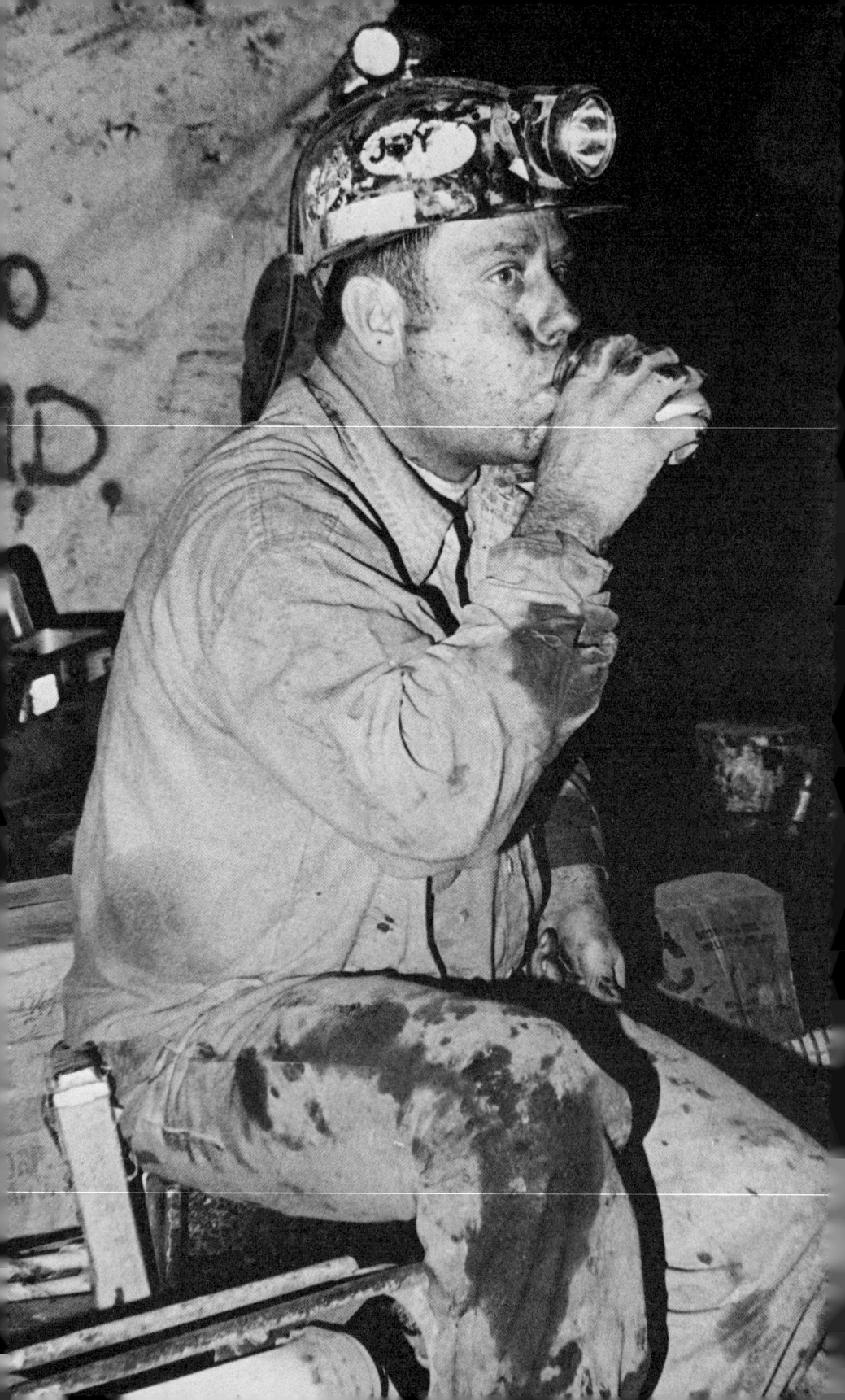

Preface

I began this book in 1975, just before leaving Appalachia for a year of study and research at the University of Chicago. My goal then was to write a book of poems reflecting coal mining life and its effects upon the people of the region.

While I was completing the manuscript, the Scotia mine explosions occurred near Oven Fork, Kentucky, where twenty-six men lost their lives. Three of those men were high school classmates of mine. Later on June 7, 1978, one of my closest childhood friends was killed in a freak accident at the United States Steel Corporation's Number 37 mine at Cumberland, Kentucky.

These events and others set a prevailing mood of death and sorrow for this manuscript.

I would have been a third generation coal miner had I not gone to college and become a teacher.

My paternal grandfather, Larkin Andrew Goode, worked in the copper mines near Copperhill, Tennessee, before he moved his family to Benham, Kentucky, to work for Wisconsin Steel Coal Mines of the International Harvester Company. There he hand-loaded coal, farmed new ground land, and reared his large family. Larkin was of "Black Dutch" origin and was a relatively short, stout, dark wavy-haired, black-eyed man. He was one of the few coal miners who could advance a breast auger six to seven feet into the coal without having to stop. My paternal grandmother, Idaho Missouri (most of my grandmother's sisters were named for states and most of the brothers for great American heroes) was Scotch-Irish by way of Northern Ireland. She was a tall, fair-skinned lady with a hot temper and easily primed tears.

PREFACE

James Skelt Parsons, my maternal grandfather, was Cherokee Indian-Irish and worked his way to the Wisconsin Steel Coal Mines by way of the railroad. A genius at repair of heavy equipment, he spent most of his life working in a shop in the Machine Shop Hollow section of Benham. My maternal grandmother, Fannie Brashear, was of French-Indian origin and was a black-haired beauty with the most radiant smile that I have seen on anyone.

Both my mother and father graduated from Benham High School, a company-owned facility. When my grandfather Goode died, my father refused a full scholarship in physics to Morehead State University to assume the role of provider for six brothers and sisters. He went to work in 1934 and forty years later retired. He was twenty-eight years old before he married and began a family of his own.

My mother, Geneva Parsons, was the oldest in a family of three girls. At a very young age she was an excellent seamstress, cook, decorator, and all-around homemaker. In recent years she has become a library assistant at Southeast Community College.

I was born August 8, 1948, the second in a family of three sisters and a brother. The home I remember was a four room company-owned shack with a mostly dirt yard and an insulation factor of R-0. The path to the outhouse grew longer every winter—especially when one had to travel it, not only for himself, but with three sisters who were scared of the dark. Life then was a series of company lay-offs and months of slack or no work. One particular winter when the mines were only working one or two days a week all we had to eat were potatoes and an occasional glass of milk.

PREFACE

Until I graduated from the eighth grade, I attended the company-owned school. Then the company sold the town to the people and the school was consolidated with a public school at Cumberland. There, in the spring of 1966, I graduated sixteenth in a class of one hundred forty-eight. During two years at Southeast Community College at Cumberland, I met my wife, Sandra Marie North, and on November 8, 1968, shortly after I transferred to the University of Kentucky at Lexington, we were married.

After graduating in 1970, I participated in the first teaching internship program ever attempted in the Commonwealth of Kentucky. Lynman Ginger, Dean of the College of Education at Kentucky, believed that one could hand pick a group of senior college students, send them directly into the public school system without conventional student teaching, and see them become successful teachers. Twenty-one of us were sent, with full pay and a commitment, into the Jefferson County Public School system in Louisville. Ninety-five percent were offered a renewal of contract for the following year. All but one received a Masters degree that summer.

In 1972 I returned to Southeast Community College, working with the Upward Bound and Special Services Program. Except for the year at the University of Chicago, I have worked with these programs for the past seven years.

In addition, I have developed a small Appalachian Studies Program, which focuses on teaching, collecting oral history, and building a photographic archive.

—James B. Goode
August, 1979

Poets of Darkness

Make them poets of the darkness,
For they speak from black faces
Lapping the sounds like red tongued dogs
Hurried after water.
We have seen them
Hunkered in the guts of steel
And we have seen their mantrips of segmented rusting cars
Being sucked and swallowed by long black holes.

Yes, make them poets
Make them hands of fossil ferns,
Give them grips on black diamond pens,
Have them speak Paleozoic languages
Decoded from Rosettas made of coal.

Make them tell us what it means to see into aeons
Where no man has seen.

Wednesday, June 7, 1978
Today the Blackest Roses Bloom

This
Too late afternoon
My Mother,
Her eyes like withering roses,
Came to me
Down the long hill to my house
And I,
At my door,
Holding an empty gasoline can
On my way to a gas station
With the smallness of my son's hand in mine,
Choked with my silence
And with numb ears
Heard you were dead.
Heard you died
While I talked next month
With the Yale professor.

Not knowing why at the time
I carried on
And in one continuous motion
Picked up the rhythm of my life again
And into the truck with my son
And down to the gas station
And back to start the mower
And mowed in the rain
Like a madman in a trance
Until wet as a river
No one could tell the tears from the raindrops
And all the while
In my mind
I saw you standing there
Between the shuttle car and the continuous miner
With your upraised hand
And unspoken words
As the killer rock slid down upon you.

I wanted to say to you then
What I had wanted to say to you every day
As we passed
Going in opposite directions.

Mike,
If I could
I would wash the black from your face,
Lift the rock from your heart,
Breathe life back into your lungs,
And make you speak to me again.
But now all I can do is embrace your widow
And the little blonde haired boy
Who stumbled down the high steps
Leading from the church
And kiss the two wide-eyed girls
You left behind
Who will know you only as a leaf
That fell ages and ages ago.

Today
The blackest roses bloom
And their shadow
Is a shadow
In the shadow
Of your tomb.

Late Afternoon

Late afternoon
At Eli Bovich's Tavern . . .
Friday,
And coal miner's trucks are parked in rows
On both sides of U.S. Highway 160.
Inside
Dilated raccoon like eyes
Watch the bouncing asses of the barmaids.
Thirsty throats pull at the foamy draft in the mugs
As coal dusted ears are mesmerized
By a concoction of Johnny Paycheck,
The bowling machine,
Laughter,
Argument,
And a dash of brooding silence
Leaned over a sweating bottle.
I go to the upper level
Next to the plywood bathroom.
Rodney Adams motions for me to sit at his table.
I'm grateful to see a face I know.
Greetings exchange—the ritual "How do you do's,
How are you's"
As I sit on the orange vinyl seat
Across the table,
My eyes still remembering outside.

A round of beer is ordered and arrives,
Splashing over the frosted mugs
As the barmaid slaps the glasses down hard
And slides them across the table.
I don't mind,
She has to lean over to wipe the foaming beer
And I glimpse the lace traveling
Her well tanned breasts.
The beer is cold

Stinging the throat
Like a slow moving ice cube does.
Something about seeing the coal miner in Rodney
Makes me want to talk about Mike.
"It's been hard for me to believe that Mike really got killed,"
I say.
"I was there . . ."
His voice trails off

Silence

His voice comes back like a pulsating signal.
"I was with him minutes before he got killed."
"It should've been me."

More silence

"It was his time to die.
If he'd a been six inches to the left or right
It would've missed his chest
And probably only have broken his legs.
But he was in the right spot at the right time.

I was standing in that same spot
Not five minutes before workin' on a pump line
But Mike sent me away
Down a couple of breaks to find some old scrap fittings
To fix a water leak with
And when I started back
I met Bill Ison, the miner operator on the section,
Running toward me in a combat Z
Dodging belt line and piles of roof bolts and cap boards
His eyes were wild as hell
and he said,
'Mike's hurt,
Mike's hurt real bad.'

And then I saw Mike lying there under the rock
and I grabbed him by the arm and shook him and said,
'Mike's not hurt, Bill
Mike's dead!'
'How the shit did this happen?' I asked him.
'I don't know,' he said.
'He turned to me and said,
'Get the miner into the coal, Bill'
and I started the miner,
Made a cut,
Turned around,
and he was under this rock."

This time a longer silence
As we both draw deep from the beer.

He continued.
"I went for the scoop
To lift the rock
But the sight of his crushed body made me sick.
I stopped and vomited in a breakthrough.
I didn't want the other men to see.
But they were all doing the same. . .
All vomiting in the breakthroughs."

"I came back with the scoop and placed the bucket under the rock
And tried to raise it.
It was a long rock,
Maybe 20-25 feet long and 2½ feet thick.
A couple of times the rock teetered on the scoop
And my heart almost quit.
I kept thinking that I didn't want to hurt him anymore
But then my own words hung in my throat.
'Mike's not hurt,
Mike's dead.' "

This time silence is too much,
I have to leave.
Late afternoon at Eli Bovich's Tavern
And night has penetrated the windows of Harlan County
    Kentucky.
My eyes have adjusted to the night.
More trucks have lined U.S. Highway 160 in Cumberland.
Thoughts of Jan, the widow, seep into my brain
As Linda Rondstat
Sings in coincidence with the moment:
"I never will marry,
I'll be no man's wife,
I expect to live single,
All the days of my life."

Song of Sorrow

They are gone,
Screaming the mine full of eagle mouths
To hook the air
With the snags of tongues.

Twenty-six coal miners dead
And four miles of night bleeds black air
Like the rhythmic time drip
Of sulfur water upon the slate.

They are gone,
But I hear them in my dreams
Pulsating visions of them alive—
A numb surrealistic parading of pictures
In a fitful night.

Where is Scottie Combs?
He lies beneath the hemlock's needle shade.
He sleeps like sandstone upon the land.
I hear his soul whisper
In the gusts of wind through filaments of grass.
I hear him falling in his dreams
And I see him dying before he wakes.

And where is Roy McKnight?
He is helpless in his grave.
He sleeps in the damp of earth and rocks
Beside the rage of Cloverlick Creek.
I see him mix with his father's dust
And resurrect the flowers.

And where is Lawrence Peavy,
Who kissed life
Like a bee kisses flowers?
He is gone to be the earth;
He has gone to speak for Africans
Who wail frightened voices
In sounds that stretch two hundred years.

Where have Boggs, Coots, Scott, Gallaway,
Griffith, Widener, Turner, Gibbs, and Sturgill gone?
They have gone
To scream a mine full of eagle mouths;
To lick clean the blackened faces of eleven
Who sleep with silent dust trails
Climbing crossing beams of light
Until they yield to hours
And fade to night.

Her Bear Branch Man

She came
In the cold blue snow
Of a Leslie County Kentucky winter morning
To claim his blackened body
Shrouded with a rubber sheet
From the floor
Of the high school gymnasium
Where he lay beside
Thirty-eight other dead miners.

Her Bear Branch man
Suddenly an insignificant, crumpled shape
Beside the bleachers
Wet with tears
Dripped like rain
From forest leaves.

Like the Last Good-Bye

The women
Kiss their miners
Like it was
The last good-bye
Never having room
For all the emptiness
Always realizing
Their backbroken,
Belly scarred men father sons
Who will fill the deep muddy tracks
To the mine
Always they
Wonder who will be the one
To kiss their son
The last good-bye.

A Funeral for Five of the Thirty-Eight Dead

Rubber
In the legs
And brains
And moans
And in the caskets
Rocking in the bosom of Abraham.
Rubber
In the Church of God
Full with
The wood of tears
And calloused knees
And coal miners singing
"They ain't no grave gonna hold my body down"
As night falls
Like a hammer
In the mountains.

Coal Miner's Graveyard

In this graveyard
Wispy sage grass leans in gentle winds
Bending and rattling like snake tails.
Jar flies buzz wafer wing sounds
While miners sleep
And wandering seeds
Are blown across the graves
Searching for a place to rest—
A place where they will uncoil
In a miner's dust
And stretch an aching for new life
Slowly toward the sun.

For Those Who Sleep

Their art awakens melancholic tributes
To their sinews—
Their voices the colored signal threads
Of mine tattoos.
And in their bodies bred from coal
We see the wrinkled past
Unroll.
And the
Zigging
Zagging
Threads
Of undulating coal scars
Run black
Across their heads.

When Coal Miners Come Home

When coal miners come home
Anxious ears listen
For the footsteps
To strike the worn wooden steps—
For the deep coughs
And the clang of
The round metal dinner bucket
Against the lap siding.

When coal miners come home
There upon the flowered linoleum
Before a glowing grate basket
Of yellow smoking coal
They slide into a mirror
Of hot water steaming in a galvanized tub
And groan signals long and painful
Like old mine timbers taking weight.

Everyone listens,
Learning how to come home—
How to signal
With footsteps striking worn wooden steps.

They Come to Dig Coal

They come to dig coal
Between the swaying cribs.
Dancing in slow motions toward the face
They float above the flat beds
Of whining battery cars.

They come to dig coal
Bearing upon their backs
A stabbing weight
To make them groan
Sounds of splintering mine timbers
In restless dreams at night.

Swift as the fall of kettle-bottoms
They move into the coal
And then retreat
With raccoon masks
And vital hands
And veins running black with dust.

Black Labyrinths

In hills of sound
Underground
Bumping coal   railroad steel rings
Cars grind   sixty pound track
Rubber tires   on mining buggys
Whine over   rolls in the bottom
Sucking fans   force air
Through black labyrinths
For miners
Who wheeze like dogs
Walk like ducks
Run like mice
To find
The cheese.

Coal Car Riders*

In austere blue snows,
August yellow suns,
Slanted needle rains,
Or morning mists that melt
Like life itself
Riding the rusted rail cars
Their dusted faces bob
Above the humps of coal
As careful creviced hands
Circle the brake wheel
Pumping danger like a strong heart.

Long eyes peer down the track
Toward the end
Waiting for the abrupt halt
In a shuddering coupling
Of coal car against coal car
When the riders can descend
With leather
Umbilical
Safety belts
Dangling
Cut from the reluctant groaning
To walk back alone
Up the long steel track.

* Some coal companies still use men instead of yard engines to move the railroad coal cars from a loading point to a side track. The miner must control the speed of the car with a wheel which is connected to a braking system.

edit: Malcolm Jay Wilson

Credit: Malcolm Jay Wilson

Credit: Vic Howard Collection, University of Mississippi

Credit: Wisconsin Steel

Credit: Wisconsin Steel

Credit: Vic Howard Collection, University of Mississippi

Credit: Malcolm Jay Wilson

Credit: Malcolm Jay Wilson

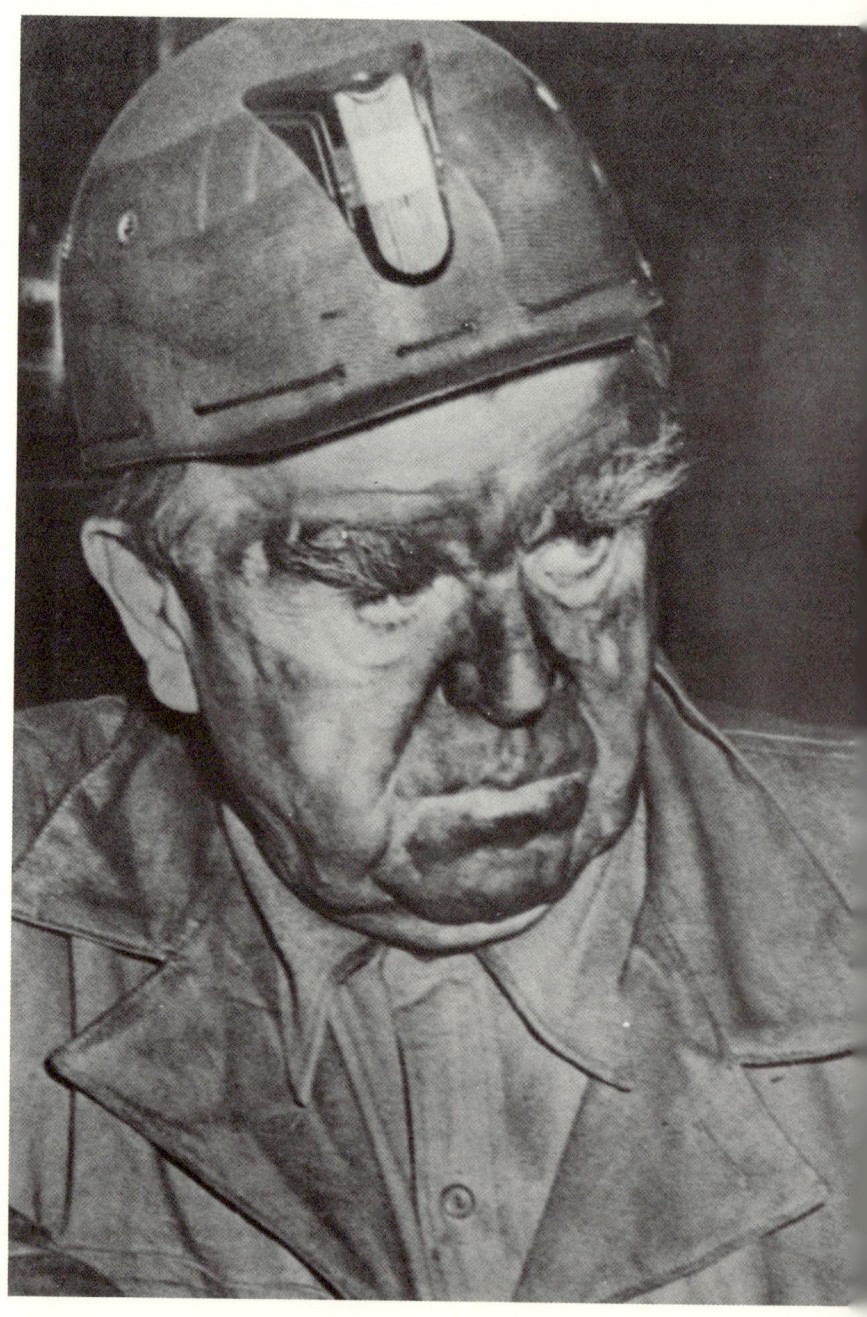
Credit: Vic Howard Collection, University of Mississippi

Where Fossil Ferns are Constellations

Under a sky
Where fossil ferns are constellations
I crawl the length of belt conveyor
As it whines a sleepy song
Turning and turning
Over the spinning of cold rollers of steel.
On all fours I crawl,
Like some worn out aging dog
Shoveling and shoveling
The thick coal dust pudding.

At last my cap light finds the end
And, having left my mind at the belt head,
I return
Letting it sink back into my dusty skull
To think of places
Where I could love you
While warm
You sleep
With your hands tucked in all our secret places.

Knowing that hell lives in these tunnels
Until the cap light finds the end,
I switch out the light,
Lean back against a wet timber,
And a million tons above this night
Where fossil ferns are constellations
The air is sweet
With the throat sounds of whippoorwills
And places
Where I could love you
While warm
You sleep.

The Coal Camp Sleeps

They sleep
Packed in dozens beneath the heavy quilts
In four room coal camp shacks
Like unsuspecting
Naked pink mice
Locked together in contorted masses
Of twined legs
And heavy mouths.

They never stir from dreams
To watch the coal squirt from holes
In the hills of night
Or to hear the morning come
With its falling
To cracked tarpaper roofs
Like black snow
And its dogs wailing like banshees
In the cold.

To a Man with a Small Truck Mine

We went,
Rolling the jeep up Montgomery Hollow
Across a bridge quivering on skinny legs
Down a mudshiny road
Where I spat out the doorless door,
My boots braced on the glove box
And you cursing fire
From your grinning face
With the dog
That kept jumping out and running in front
And looking back with his ears
To see if we were following...

We went,
Sliding along
Beside stacks of two foot mine timbers
Where you laughed
When I thought they had been cut for firewood
And I frowned when we saw the two foot mine
And the homemade shuttle car
Dragging its muddy cable
With the lean tall dirty man
Hugging the greasy metal sides
With a dripping black ton
Sleeping on the banged front bed.

We went,
From the hard look he threw our way
As he flipped his P.A. butt
Down the makeshift
Tin wood topple leg tipple slide
And the sparks flew on the wind.

You said the only way you'd do it
Would be to have a starving wife
And hungry kids at home
And all the way down the hollow
I was saying in my voiceless mind
That this was what he was doing
All dirty faced with calloused hands and arms
Hugging his way through the mud
On that cold December day
When everyone else was Santa Claus.
And as we rolled out of Montgomery Hollow
He stared into my smug warm eyes
And I into his cold, hungry, dust covered
Flat tire face.

Boom Town Boys

With baboon circled eyes
They stream from the mines
Into the night
Licking up Saturday night
Like it was molasses cornbread
Gulping whole
The boom town bars
The Star,
Red Clay,
Green Gables,
And Golden Nugget
Frying neon signs
Like eggs
In hot grease.

Boom Town Poolroom

With castanets killed
Martinez Ramirez,
Bastard Spanish one
Of the tired,
The poor,
Sweeps spit from the poolroom floor
Racks colored plastic balls
To the tune of cracking noises
And miners yelling, "RACK!"
Scoops dimes from the tattered felt
Like a hand in a game of jacks.

Beer foam flies to tobacco spattered tiles
Blown from the frosted mugs
By Boom Town boys
And the bastard Spanish one
Of the tired,
The poor,
Sweeps the disappearing foam from the poolroom floor
While Check pills rattle
Like snake tails
In Boom Town.

Roadhouses

All night the Green Gables
And Star nightclubs
Along the riverside
Reeked full of baboon-eyed coal miners
Swearing Almighty God
From hot mouths dripping with rotgut whiskey
And Camel cigarettes.
All night
Ass wiggling whores
Syruped the tables
With their beet red tongues
Licking over the lip-sticked lips
And decaying teeth
And the miners laughed
And flirted
And cursed
And bought another round
And killed each other
With gristle grins
Of bristle faces
Hot from the heat of pistol barrels
And they went back to the black hole
In the morning
And down to raise
Holy hell
At night.

The Ballad of the Harlan County Criminal Justice System

Well they took me right down to the Harlan courthouse
And they treated me worse than they'd treat a louse

Sing pie die diddle I day
Pie die diddle I day

All I'd done was steal some bread
Just tryin' ta keep my family fed

Sing pie die diddle I day
Pie die diddle I day

They sat me down in the old courtroom
And I felt my fate had come too soon

Sing pie die diddle I day
Pie die diddle I day

The very first man they called to the stand
Was charged with killin' with his bare hand

Sing pie die diddle I day
Pie die diddle I day

The old judge smiled and said to him
What ya doin' here my friend Jim?

Sing pie die diddle I day
Pie die diddle I day

Well he smiled right back from the witness stand
As the jury looked on like a twelve piece band

Sing pie die diddle I day
Pie die diddle I day

After all the testimony was said and done
The jury went out and come back in a run

Sing pie die diddle I day
Pie die diddle I day

The foreman said, "You're guilty, son!"
And I thought for sure that man was done.

Sing pie die diddle I day
Pie die diddle I day

The judge cleaned his nails with his pocket knife
Then he sentenced that man to twenty to life

Sing pie die diddle I day
Pie die diddle I day

Then he suspended the sentence in the very same breath
And it tickled that man right to death

Sing pie die diddle I day
Pie die diddle I day

The bailiff then he called my name
And I knew I'd become the object of the game

Sing pie die diddle I day
Pie die diddle I day

The lawyer screamed and tore his clothes
And I felt just like a hot rubber hose

Sing pie die diddle I day
Pie die diddle I day

The jury left and they's gone a long while
And the sweat on my head began to bile

Sing pie die diddle I day
Pie die diddle I day

And then the jury they's led back in
To tell iffin' I's goin' ta the pen

Sing pie die diddle I day
Pie die diddle I day

The foreman said, "You're guilty as hell—
I'd recommend ridin' him on a rail!"

Sing pie die diddle I day
Pie die diddle I day

Well the judge agreed and he looked mighty strange
As he gave me twenty at LaGrange

Sing pie die diddle I day
Pie die diddle I day

There's a lesson to learn about Harlan County
You can't steal bread for your family
But you can kill a man and go scot-free

Sing pie die diddle I day
Pie die diddle I day

Ballad for a Union Man

Come gather 'round boys
And a story I'll tell,
Of how the coal miners
Have suffered in hell,
Of how they've been beaten
And stripped of their pride,
All because the coal company
Was rotten inside.

When they were all young men
They were oh so strong,
They thought that the coal mines
Could do them no wrong.

So they carried the big timbers,
And the shovel and pick,
And they slaved and sweated
'Till they nearly were sick.

They breathed in the coal dust
And they coughed way down deep,
'Till they wheezed in the morning
And they wheezed in their sleep.

They fell 'neath the rock piles
And their blood they did shed
And the widows were left
To bury the dead.

They made a few dollars
But were always in debt,
For the companies had ways
Of makin' it easy to get.

The babies were born,
'Bout one every year,
And the more in the family,
The more the company they'd fear.

Afraid that they'd send them
On down the road,
With babies a starvin'
And worries, a load.

Then along came John L. Lewis,
With his voice and his eyes,
And he swatted down companies
Like common house flies.

He brought in the union,
With its power and its clout,
And cured all the miner's worry and doubt.

Now the lowly coal miner
Can be tall and be proud,
For the way he counts wages
Is with the rest of the crowd.

The fight for the miner
Has been a hard road,
It's one that's not waning,
It's one that's not slowed.
So rise to the line boys!
And don't let them get by,
For the scabs they will ruin you,
In the sweet by-and-by!

100 Days and Counting . . .

I remember one time
Down at the U.M.W.A. Local 19
In Harlan County
The miners gathered like
A colony of war ants
With their "MACK" and "CAT" hats
Flashing
In an unusual winter sun
To hoist a hurriedly
Hand scribbled
House paint sign
Declaring:
"By God if Taft and Hartley want the Goddamn
Coal mined let them come down here and mine the shit!"
And beside it another one was nailed
With the black paint still dripping down the long letters:
"Dear Jimmy Peanut Carter:
We sure as hell would like to see your ass
On a continuous miner!"
NO CONTRACT = NO WORK
100 DAYS AND COUNTING . . .

Plug-Uglies in Harlan

They came to Harlan,
Dragging their serpent tongues
Across the polish of blue pistol barrel sights,
To suck power from the fists of big Sheriff John Henry;
To take some steel from his eyes for their souls;
To rub their minds raw with the sandpaper of his voices.

And they killed
The bodies of men,
The insides of widows,
And the mouths and bellies of children.
And they killed America,
Weighting her down
With lead from the pain of bullets—
Crushing her hips until her womb
Shot forth from her thighs
Like the coal bursting from seams
Under the burden of mountains.

The Value of It All

Where is the value in the places
Where the blackened faces hide
Laughing in the drumming echoes
Of abandoned bathhouse walls?

And where is the meaning in the places
Where the empty railroad tracks
And kudzu laces
Make crazy patterns on the soil?

And the reason in the places
Where the rotting rawhide laces
From a hundred miners' boots
Are strewn upon the floor?

And the worth of blacksmiths' shops
Filled with rusted broken shovels
And the silence of the forge?

And the places where we can stand
And see the weathered safety signs,
The cracking concrete blocks,
The peeling paint,
Forgotten roofbolts,
Dead mining machines,
And the long deserted hall?

And what is the value
Of wondering about
The value of it all?

Ghost Town of Appalachia

The reasons are settled
In the greying wood
Of rusting coal camp houses
And deep within the drips of dark
In sulfur water mines
For here they wept and cried
Laughed and lived
And died.

The reasons are creviced
Into hands and faces—
A saga old as Genesis.
In their graves they stir
The eyes of those who see
The sandstone names and epitaphs
Sanded smooth by wily winds.

Paradox

In the cool of evenings
He hoes the rows
And hangs the glittering pie pans
To fox the crows.

Bringing the earth to hungry roots
His gooseneck hoe
Sings away the shoots
Of ragged weeds
And bits of jagged rocks.

In days of night
He mines the coal
To feed the mouths
Who bear his soul.

Striking the vein
His hammer sings away
The blocks of paradox
In ragged rocks.

Appalachian Snake Handlers

The beat starts slow
And the rhythm is like rain
And the old man in the back
Taps his cane

The snakes start to rattle
In their wire cage box
As they conjure up the spirits
With their wild drum knocks

And faster goes the music,
Faster goes the time,
Then the chills start coming
Up and down your spine

And wilder goes the beat
And wilder is the frenzy
As it taps its feet

Then the hands go slowly
Down into the snakes
And a few deadly minutes
Is all it takes

Then out comes the snake
Across his hand
As it dances to the beat
Of the spirit's band.

Spider

The spider web of hills
Bend
And curl around the wind
And breathe
Through tree sound
And the coal lies
Under the ground
All quiet
And silent
And abound
With black.

Grey sandstone cliffs
Breed green moss
And snake spotted sunlight
Comes across the leaves fallen
Around rotted chestnut timber.

Melted sunsets drip
Behind thorny locust trees
Where wild grapes lie black against
The tendril gyres
And the mind never tires
Of seeing an infinity of hills.

Here stands the first house upon this land,
Its hand hewn greying
Mud chinked
Poplar logs
Surrounded by the slate
And coal sludge ponds.
Its yellow poplar sides
Splashed by grey cake icing mud.
The machinery whines rip
The privacy of its aged mood.
Its fireplace mood

Where crickets should be the one to sing
Not mining belt
And hammer ring.

This is the hollow
Of my ancestor's dreams.
It is so long and rocky
It seems.
The empty buildings are immense
With quiet

Only violated by the slate
And my passionate cry
Echoing through a strange
Impending night.

These hills,
These lonely hills
Where God's own breath
Would be taken by the sight—
Where towns come together
And all that is
Is nature sounds
And quiet.

But the spider stays
Luring into its trap
Of days of nights
And nights of days
The men on whom it preys
And the spider web hills
Bend
And curl around the wind
And breathe through tree sound
And the coal will never again

Lie under the ground
All quiet
And silent
And abound
With black.

Pentecost in Coal Town

With almost total night
In Coal Town
We sat in the old 1959 Ford
Outside the church
Listening to their holy heart muscles
Crashing together like cymbals
And feeling the nervous lips tambourine
With the Holy Spirit.

Inside the cotton dresses cracked and spun
Like hot corn.
Legs jerked and jumped to paw the air.
The children of God perched and walked on the ridge of
    pews
With dry tongues licking imprints on the air
And then they collapsed
On the oil stained floor.

Lost hair pins twisted on the vibrating floor boards.
Knee length hair danced to the air like snakes.
Tears stuck to rivulet ridden faces
And voices went hoarse
With praises of God.

C Seam Shovel

Shovel with your mind, boy!
Shovel with your hands.
Shovel in your dreams
Of the angel bands.

A C seam shovel holds a lot of coal
And the weight grows heavy
As sins in your soul.

Gob all that slate, boy!
Clean about the floor.
Drill and tamp the holes
To blast down more.

Shovel in the dust, boy!
Breathe it in your lungs.
Speak as your brothers
With black diamond tongues.

Put a hand on the handle, boy!
Put the other on the shank.
Be a rhythm in the darkness
Of the creeping dank.

Drip from your brow, boy!
Drip upon the slate.
Fulfill God's promise
At Eden's gate.

Cold Beer on Hot Harlan County Nights

(For Brian Wooley and Ford Reid's *We Be There When the Morning Comes*)

You were there
When the morning came to Harlan County
Snapping your ballpoints
And cameras
Like mud turtles snappin' dead sticks—
Looking for those Brookside/Highsplint
Backward, disadvantaged, culturally deprived,
Ignorant, hillbilly, coal miner rebels
On strike for what America
Was supposed to guarantee.

You were there
Looking for the answers up Clover Fork
And finding them stark as birch limbs
On the tongues of the Junior Deatons
And Louie Staceys—
Finding them in the "Direct, unashamedly emotional
Forceful way
Mountain people come to terms
With who owns what,
Who profits from whom,
And who pays what price
To get what wage
While others rake in avalanches of profit."

And you were there
When morning came to Benham
Looking for the answers.
Where you came in a dusty Volvo,
Sat on my porch
While katydids sawed wings
On sycamore limbs
And the sweating bottles of cold beer
Disappeared
On hot Harlan County nights.